# Butterflies

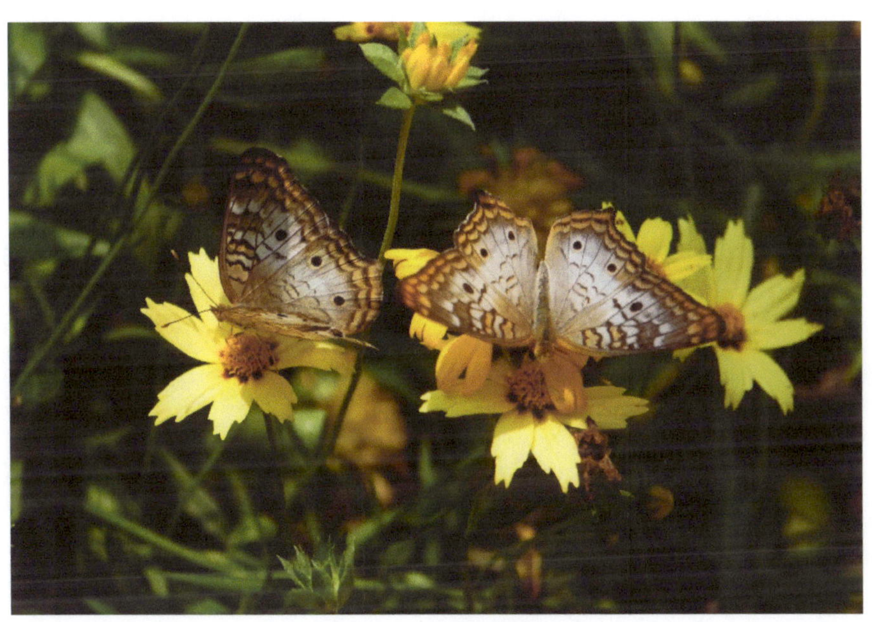

Kristen Arbour

Butterflies



**ISBN-13: 978-1976594823**

**ISBN-10: 1976594820**

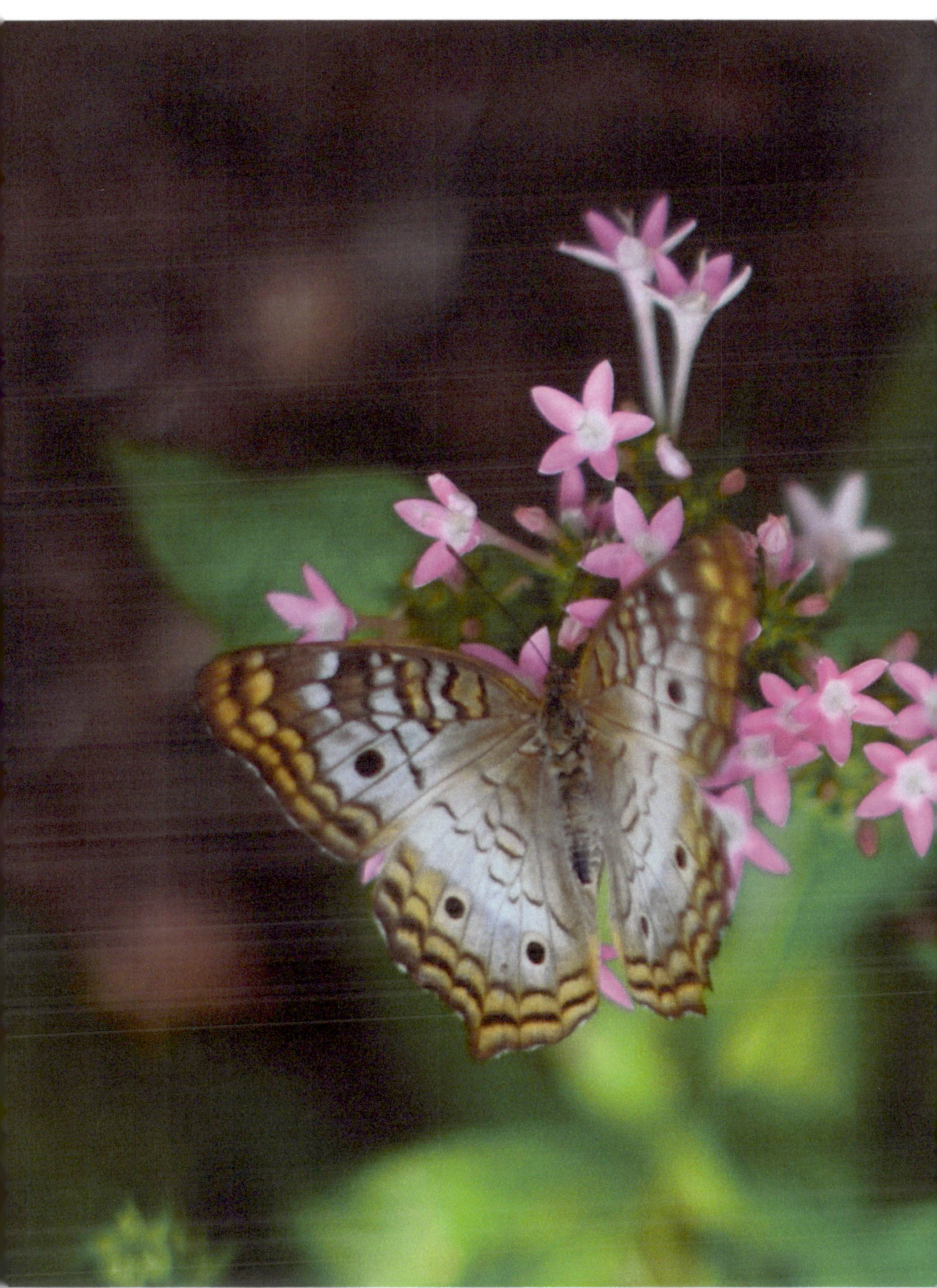

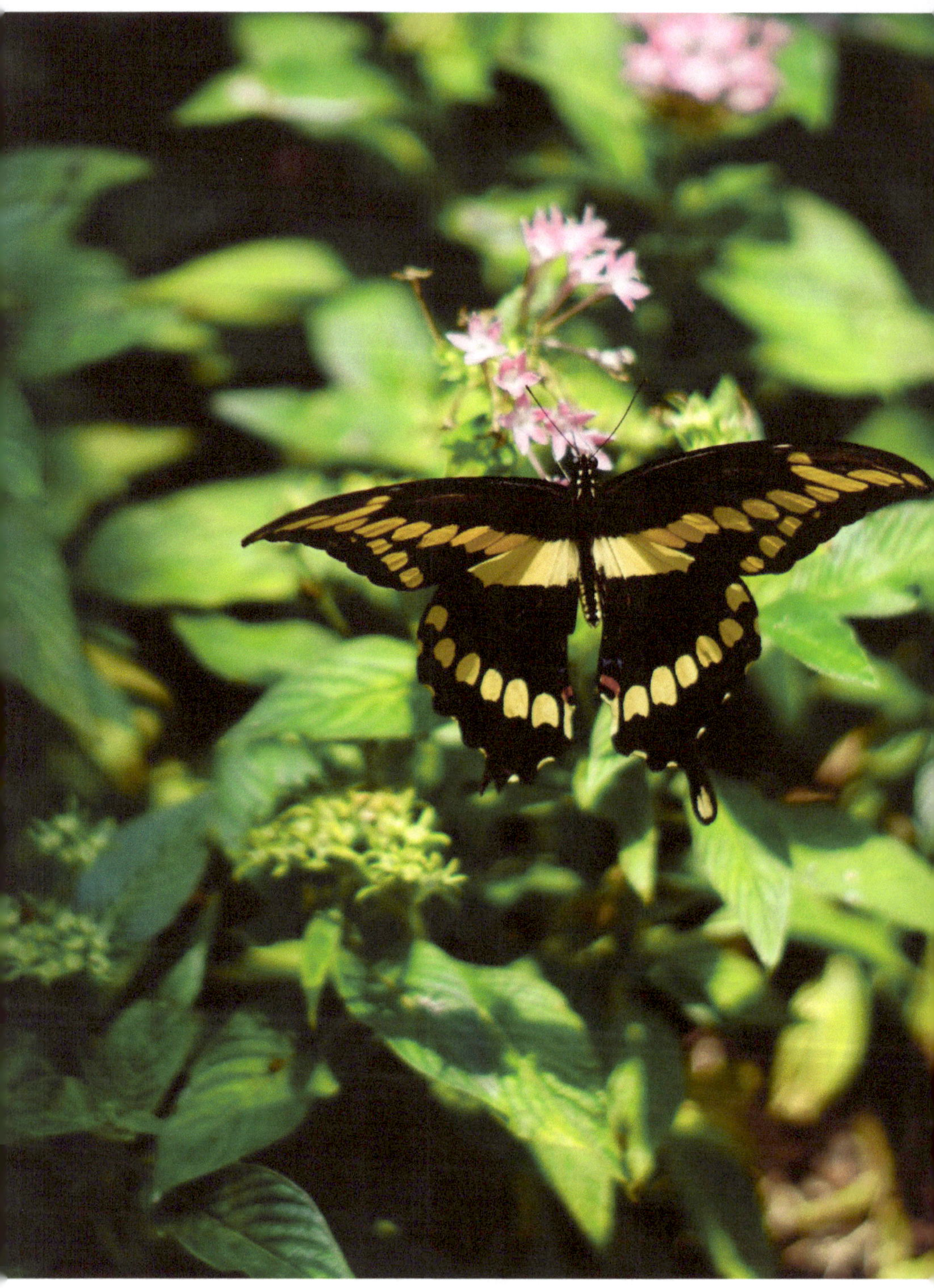

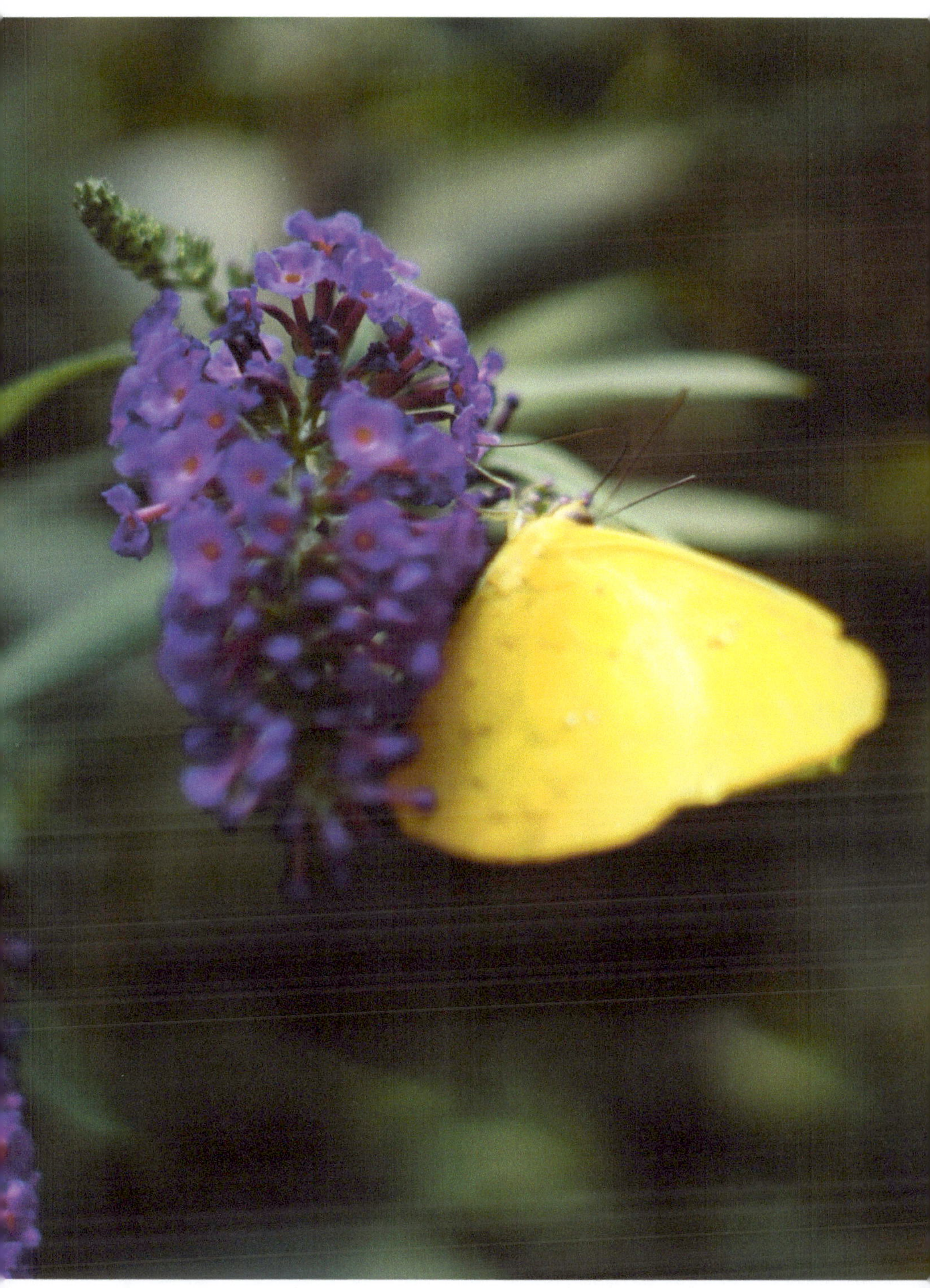

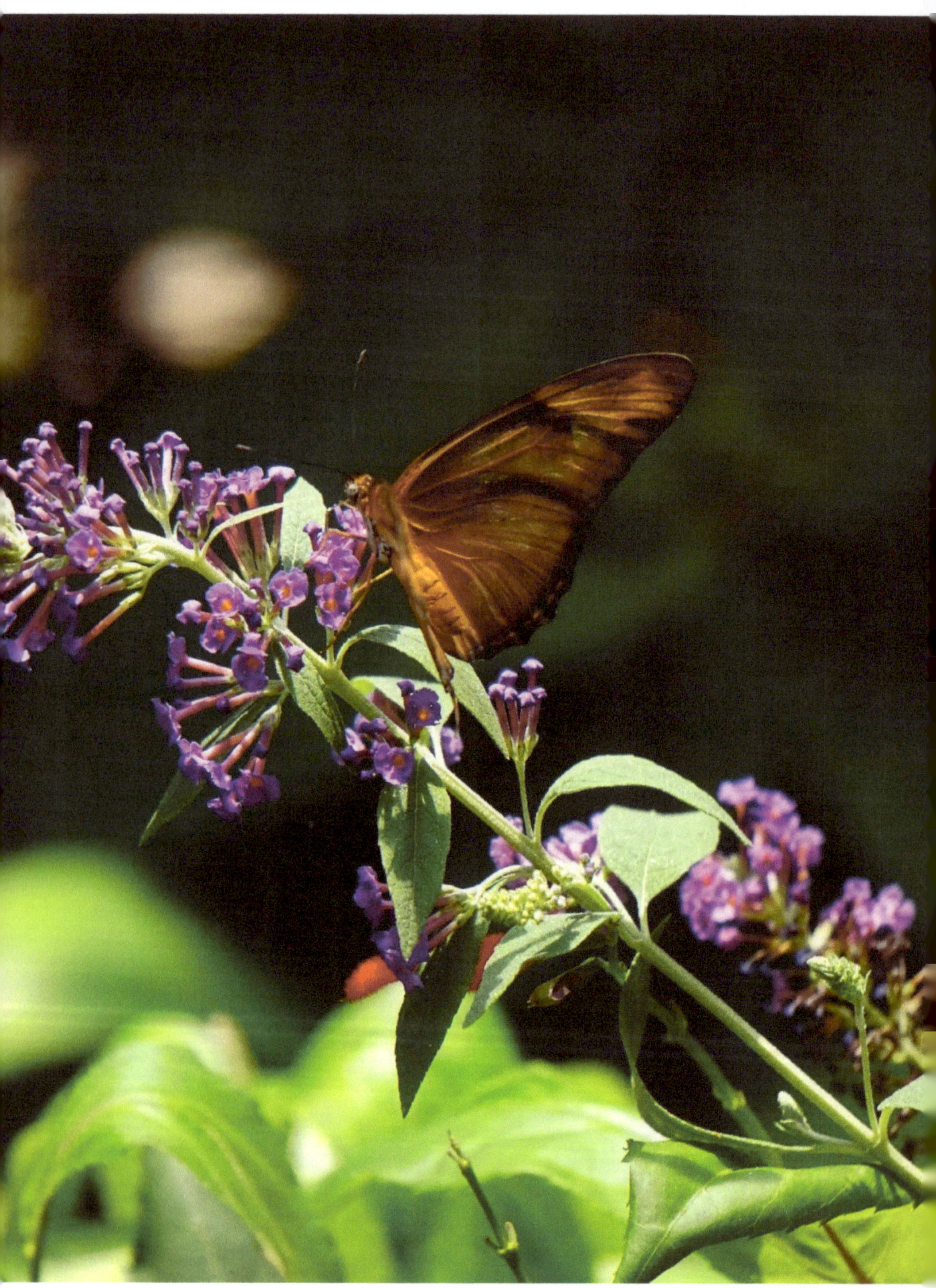

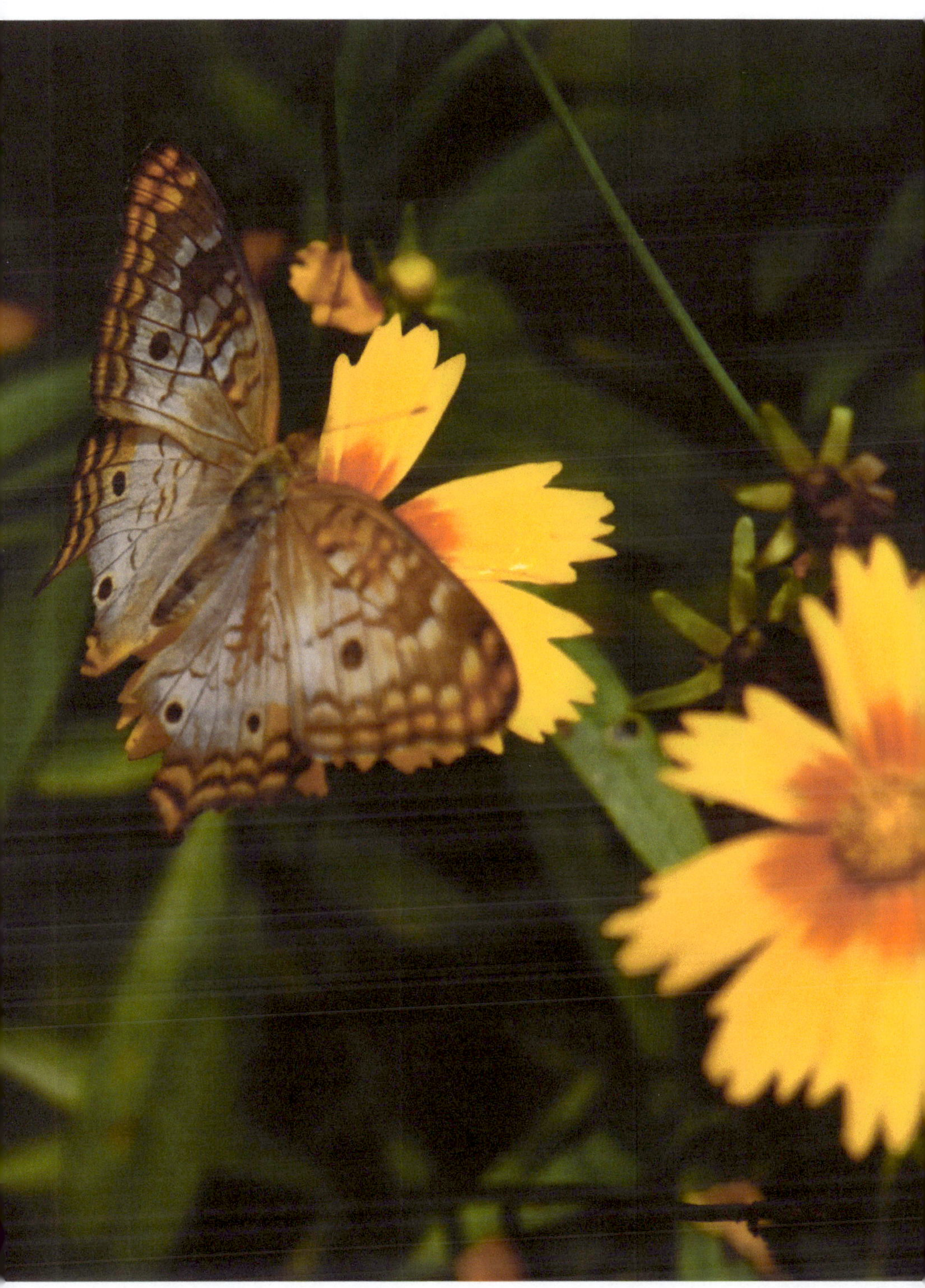

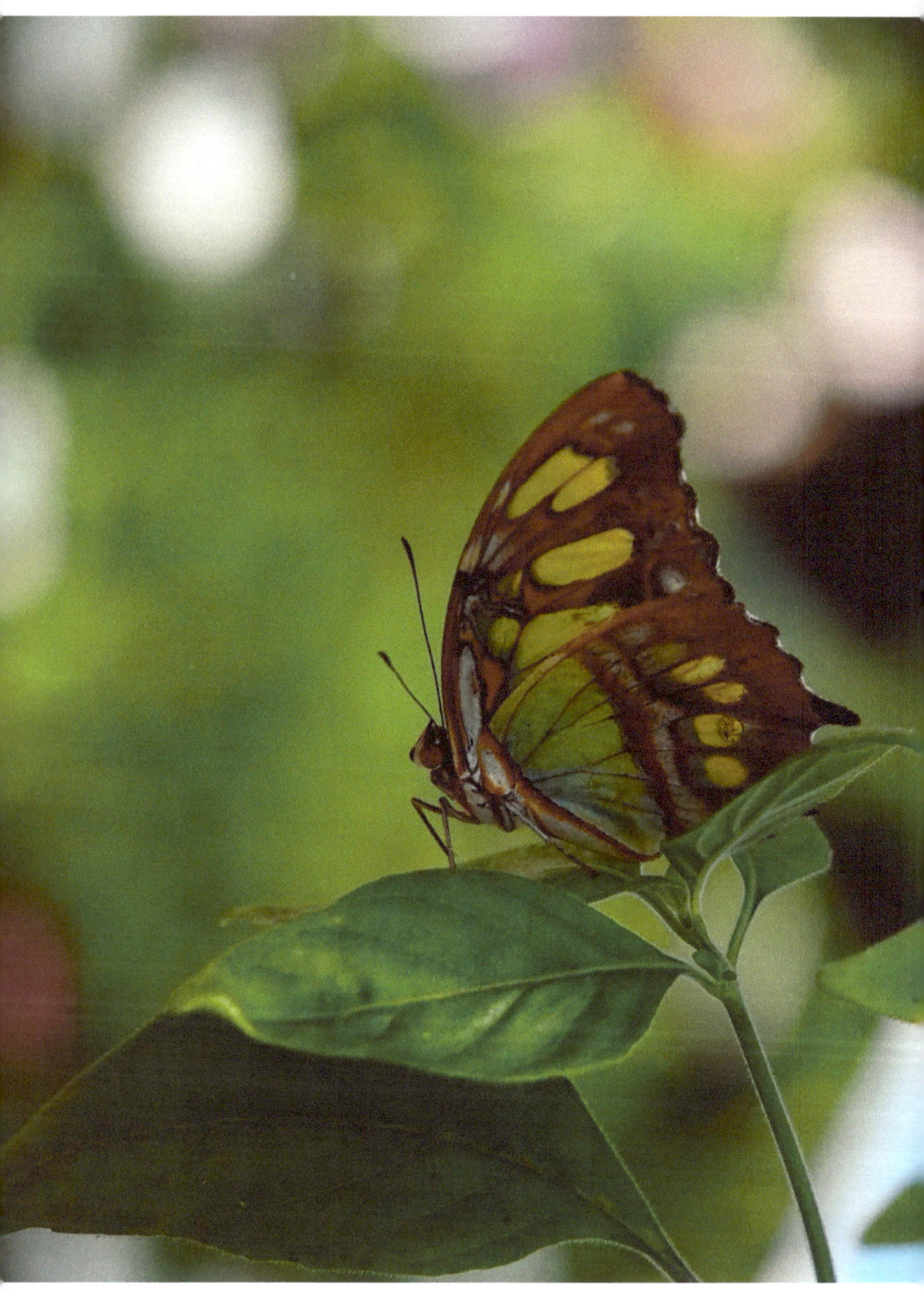

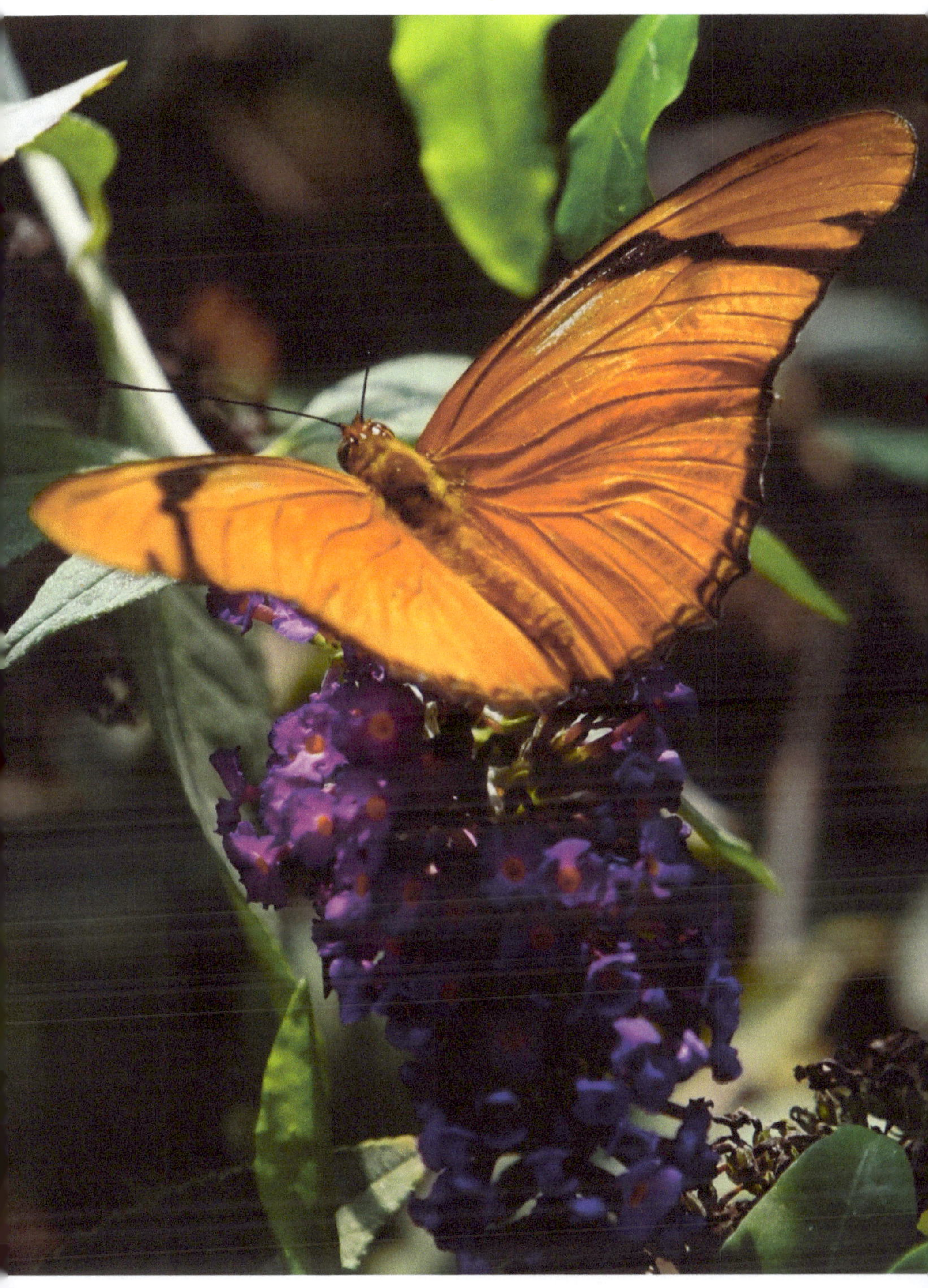

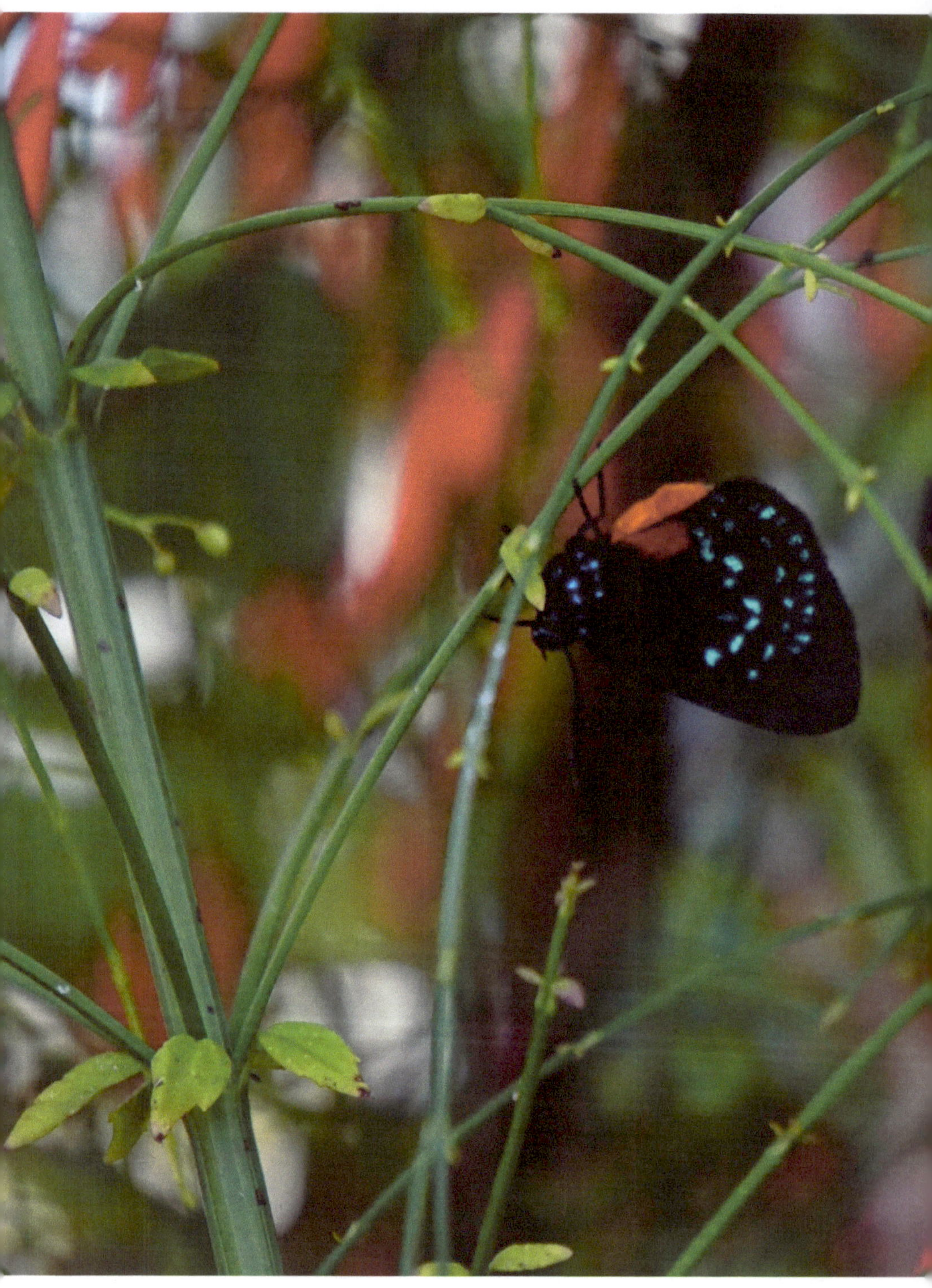

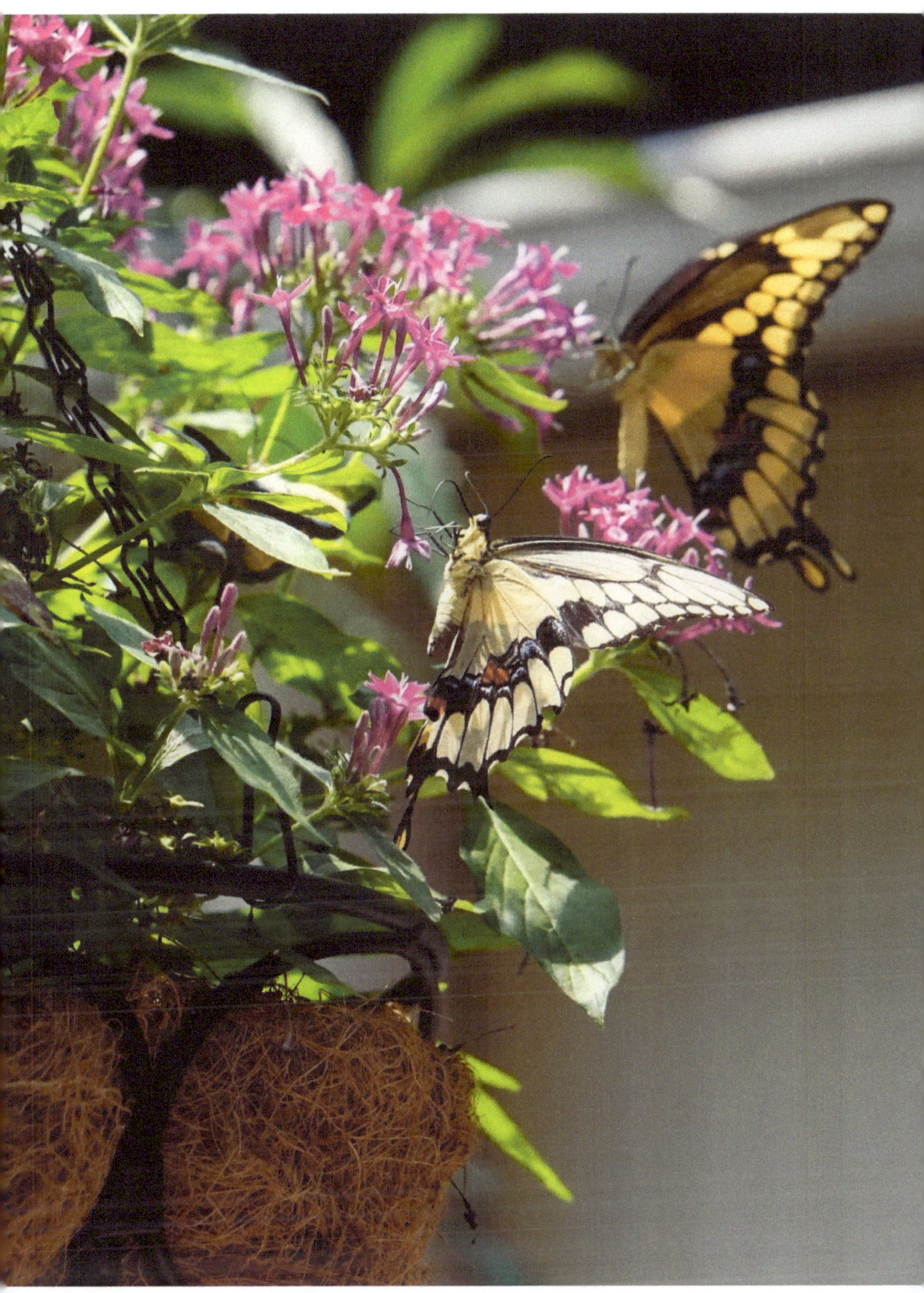

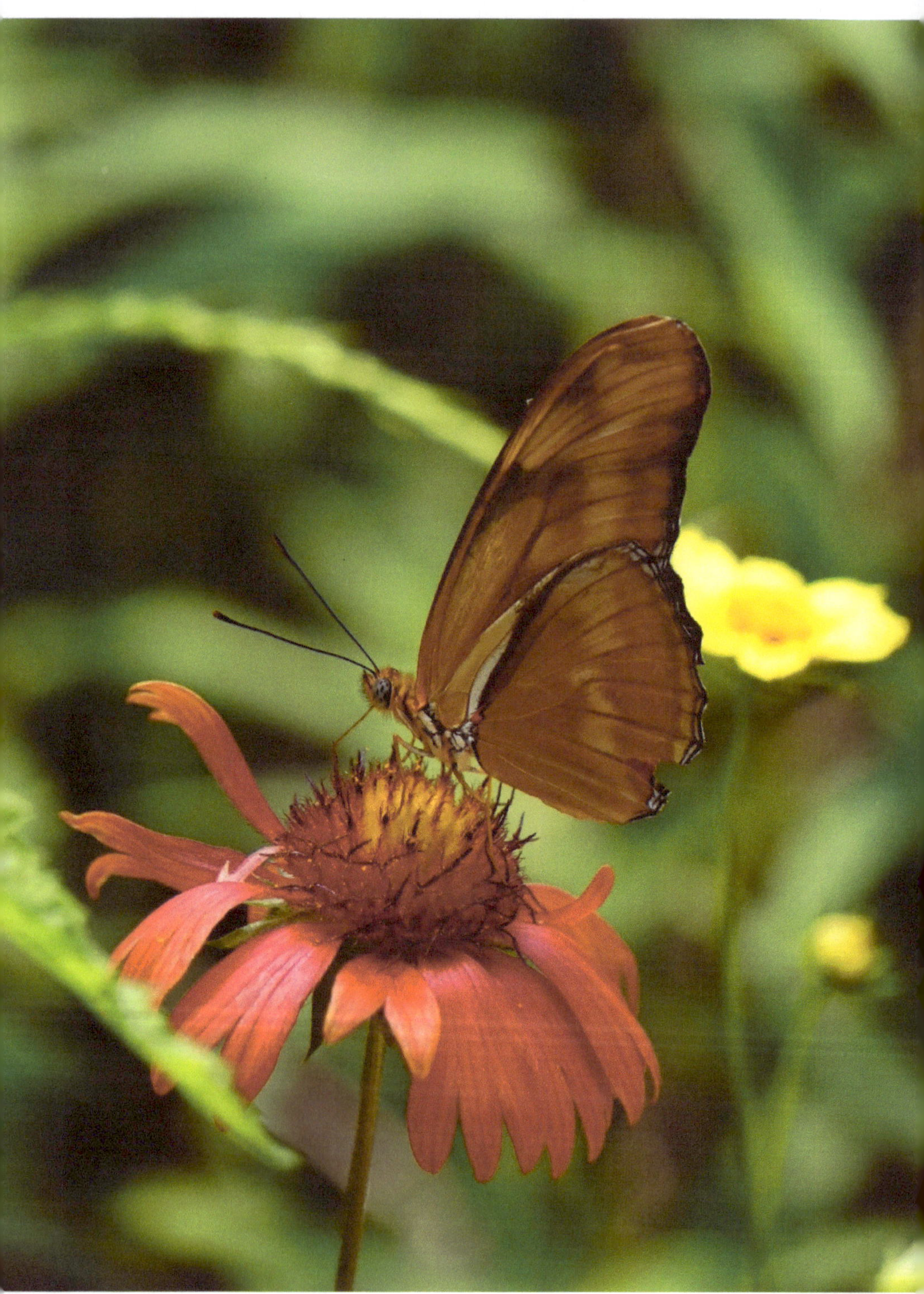

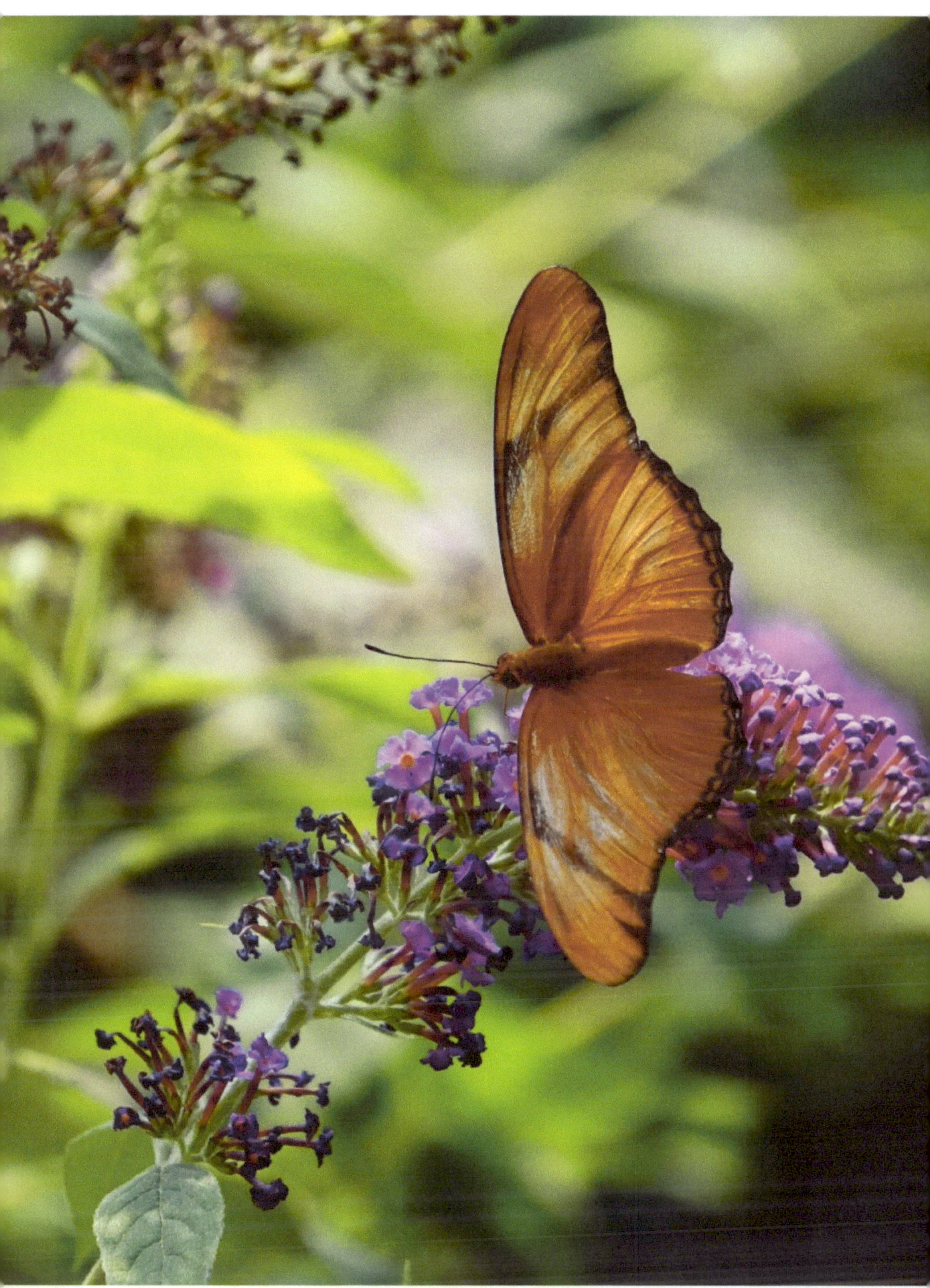

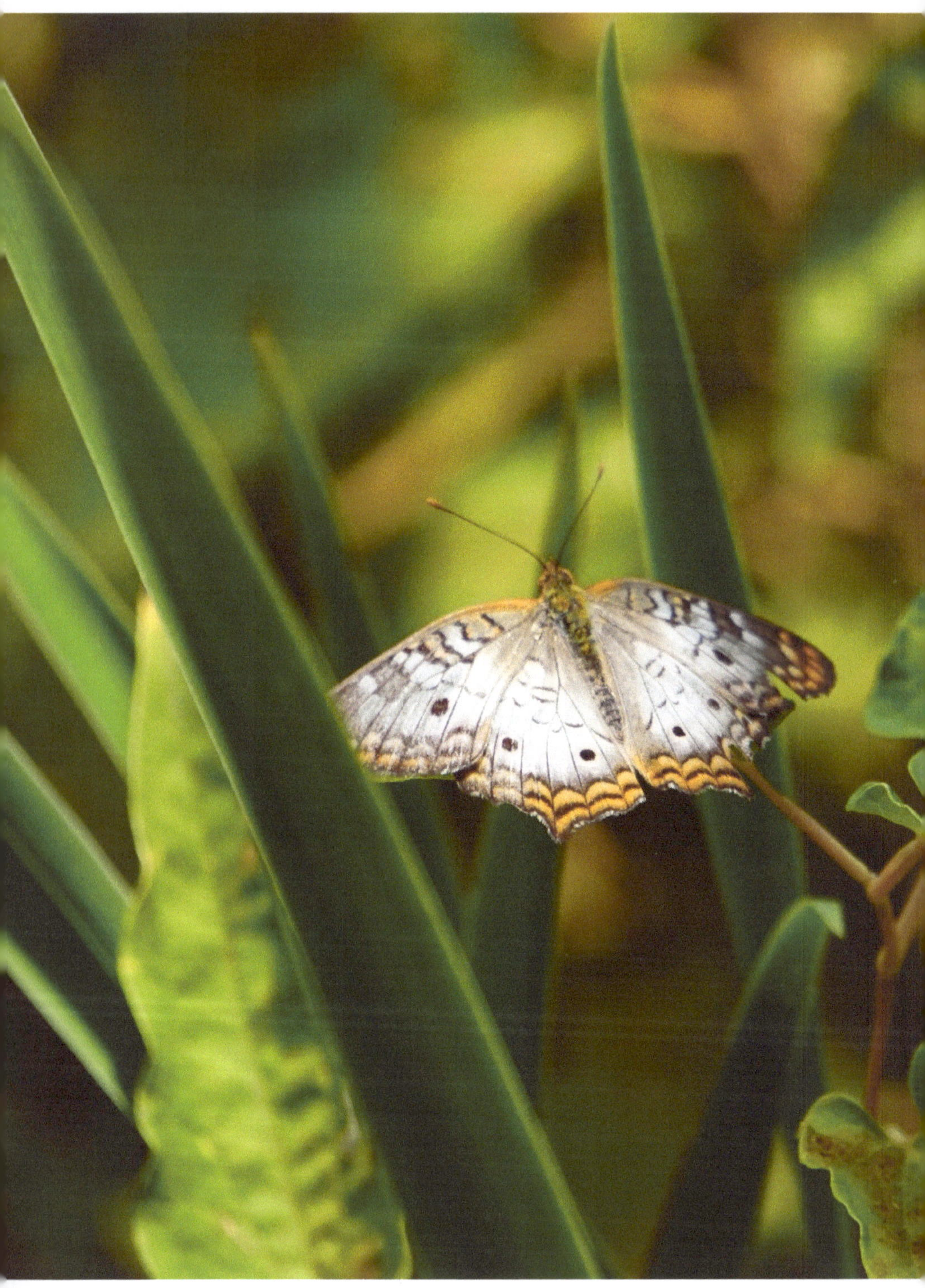

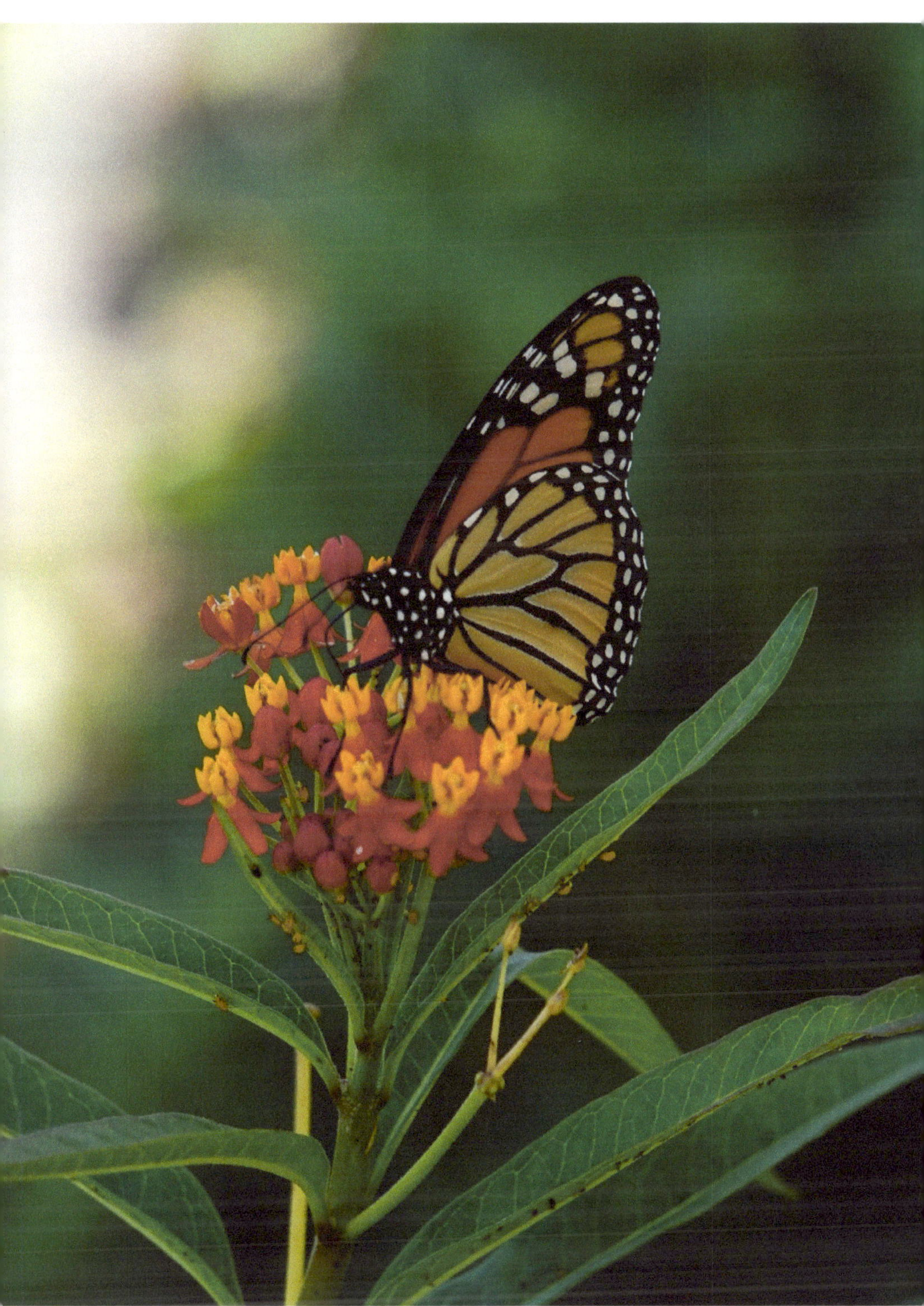

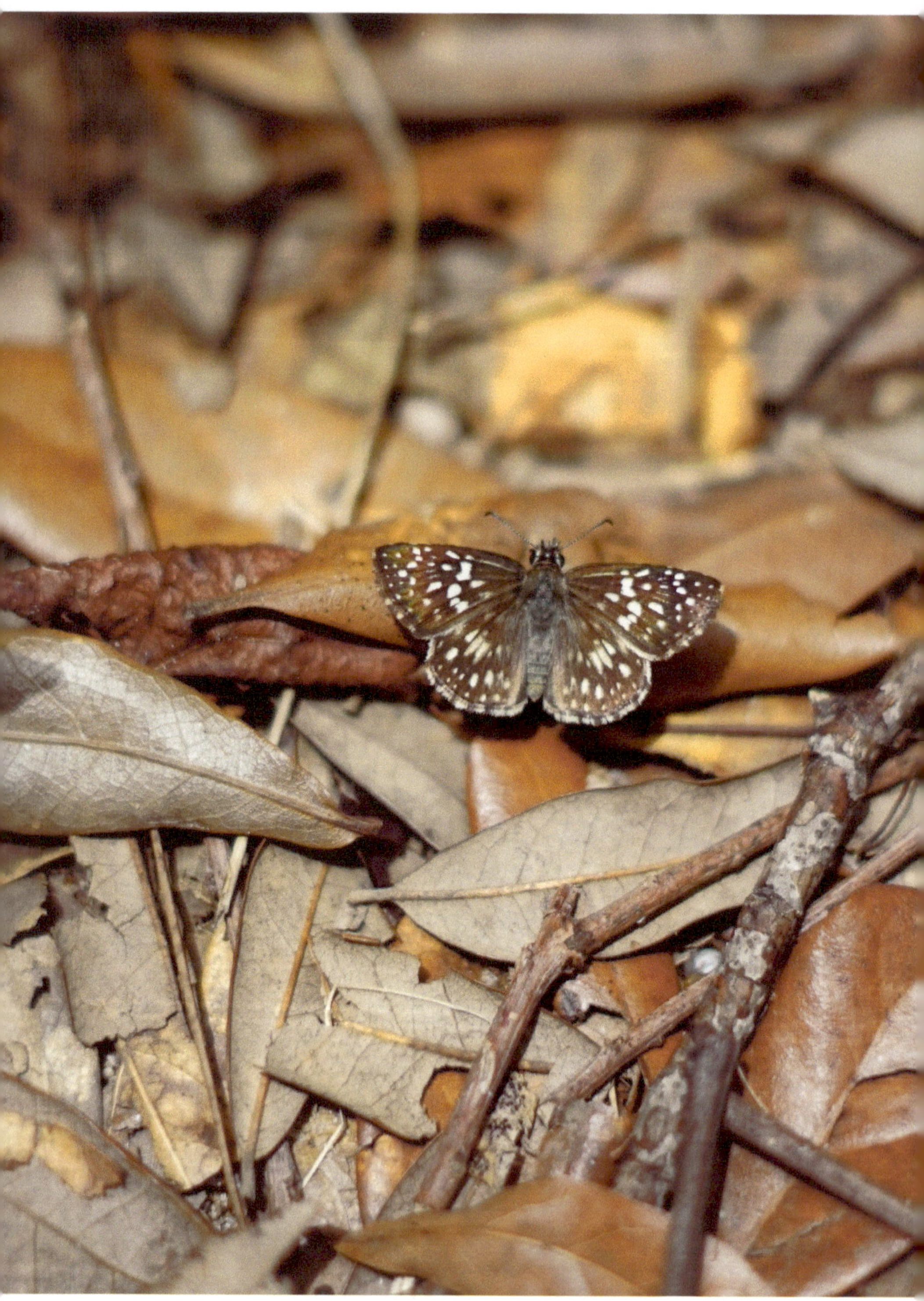

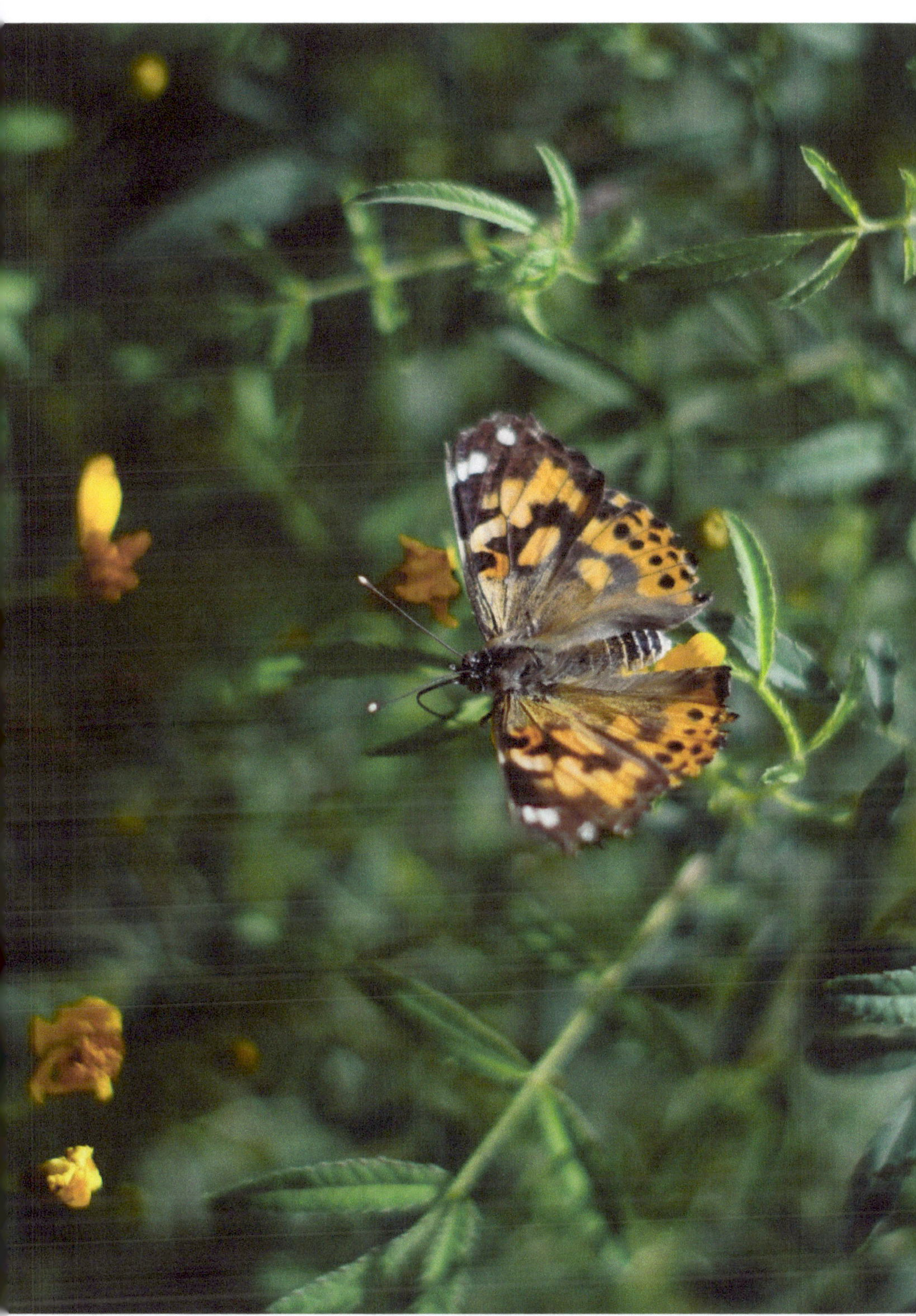

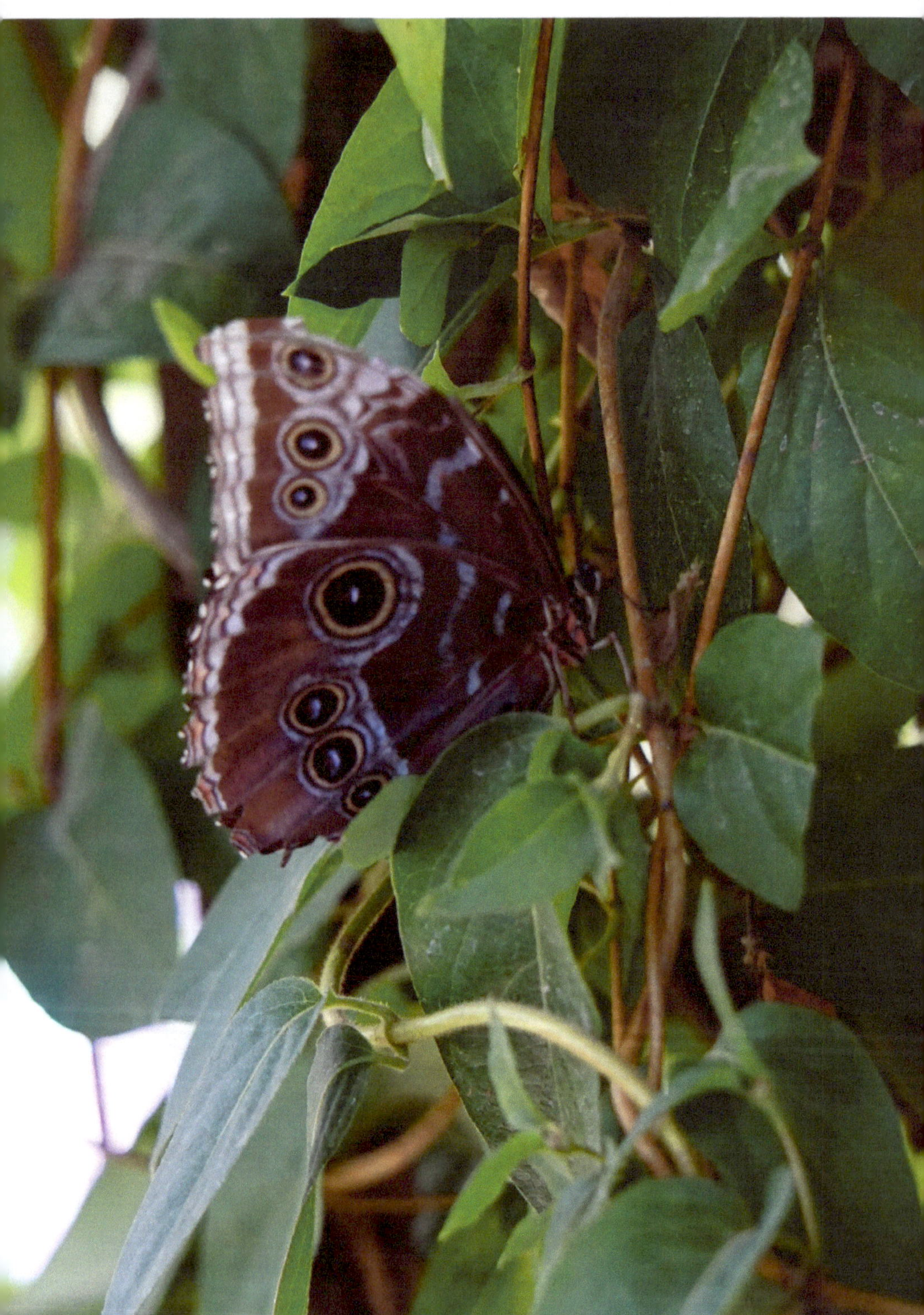

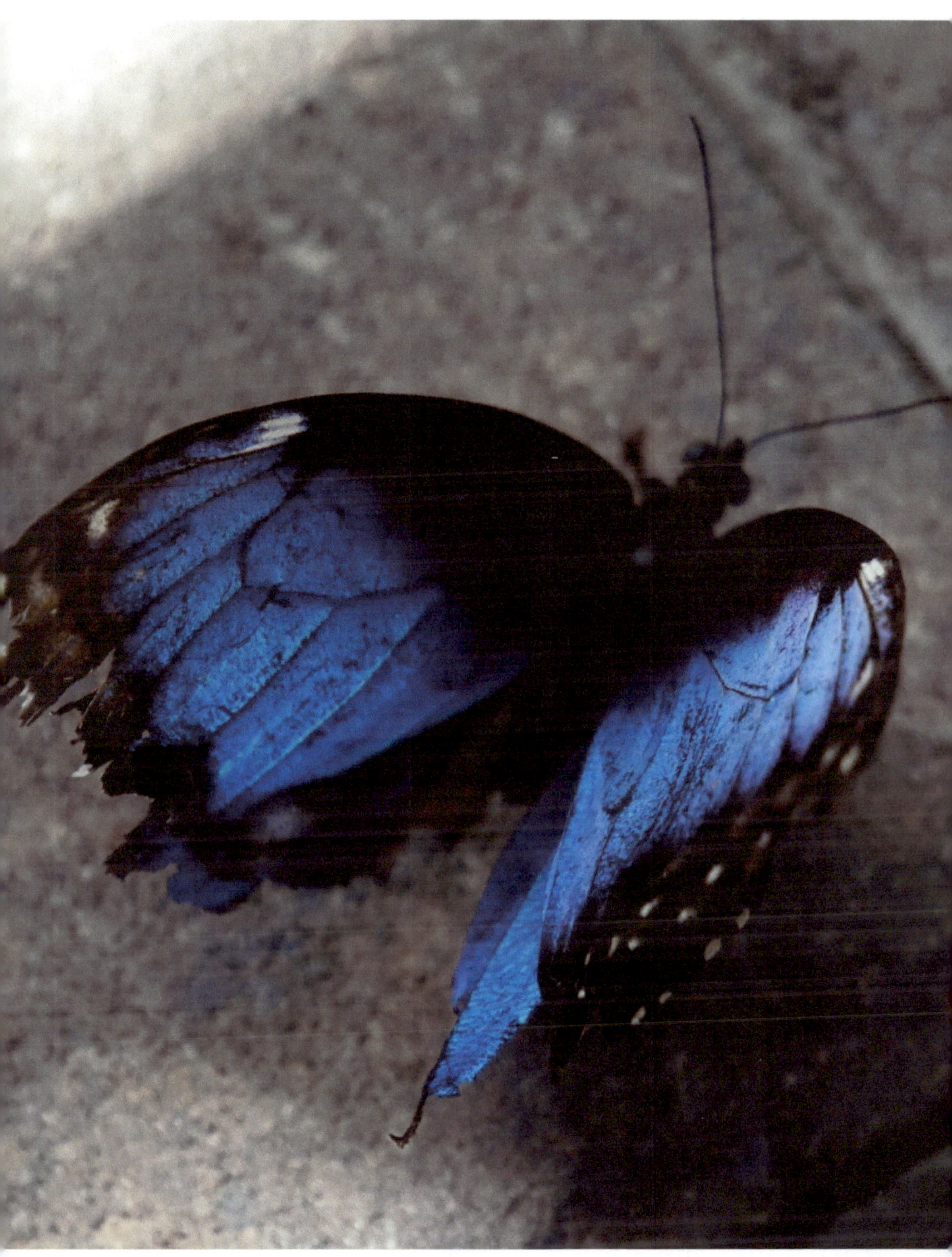

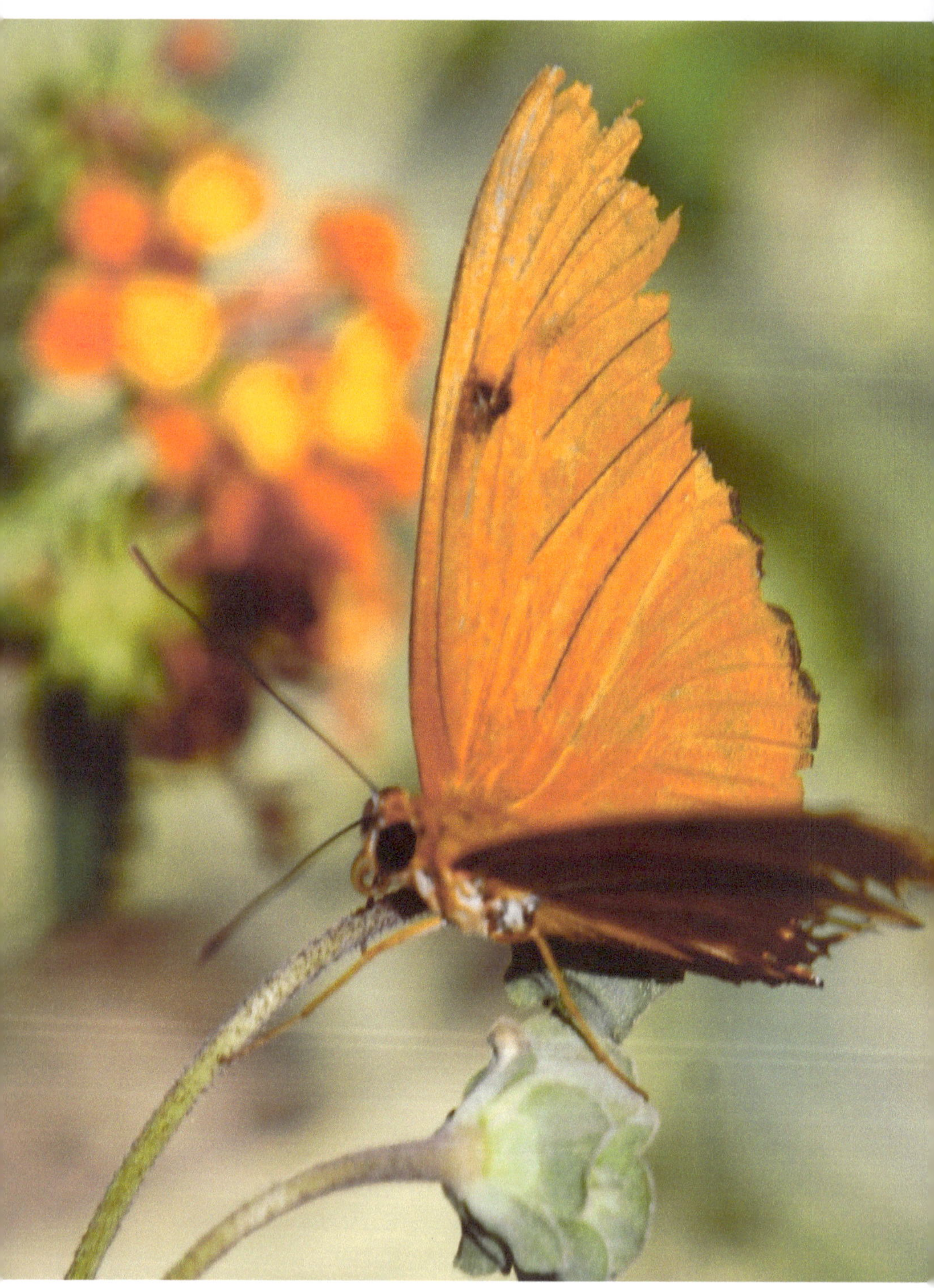

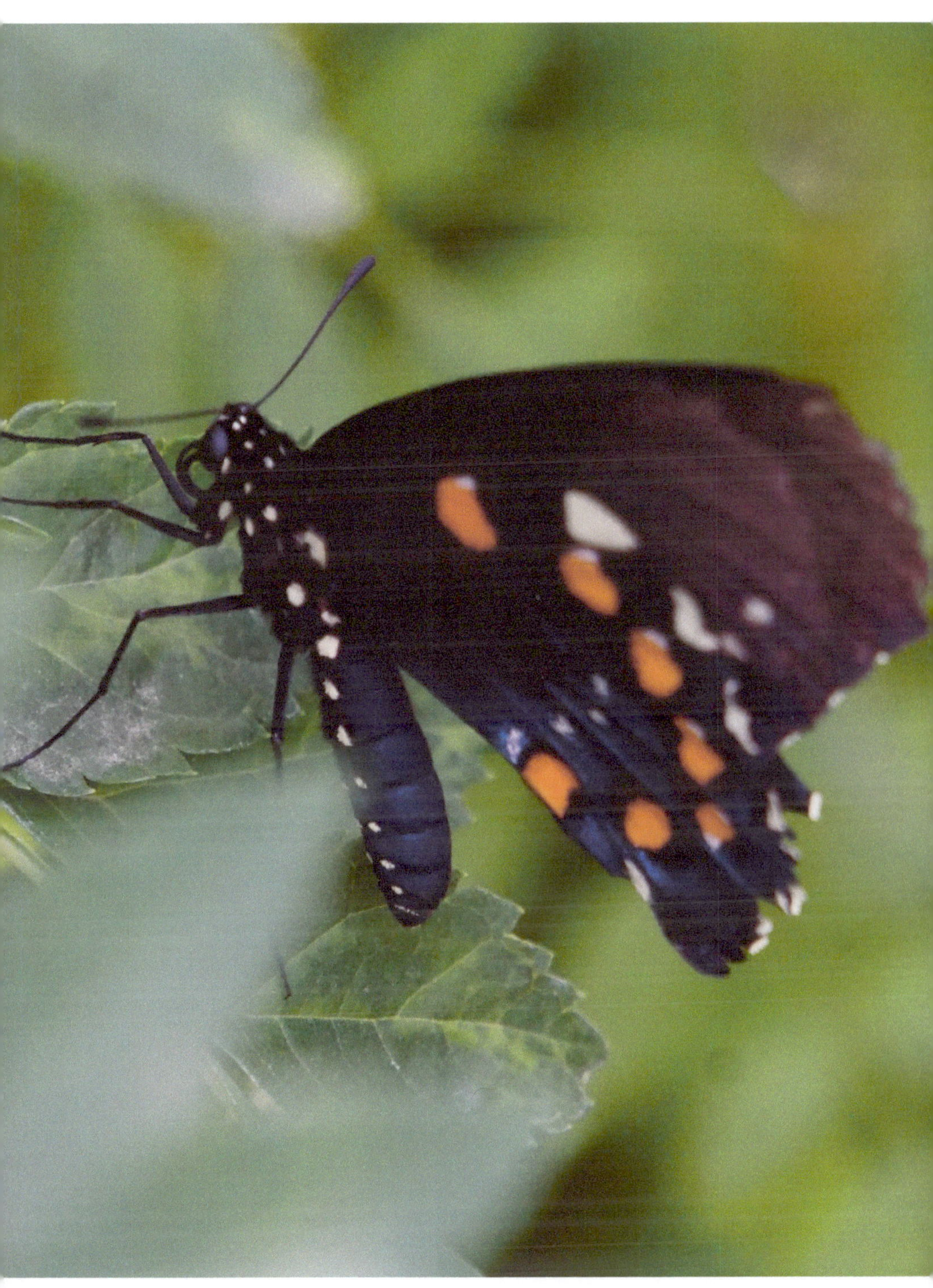

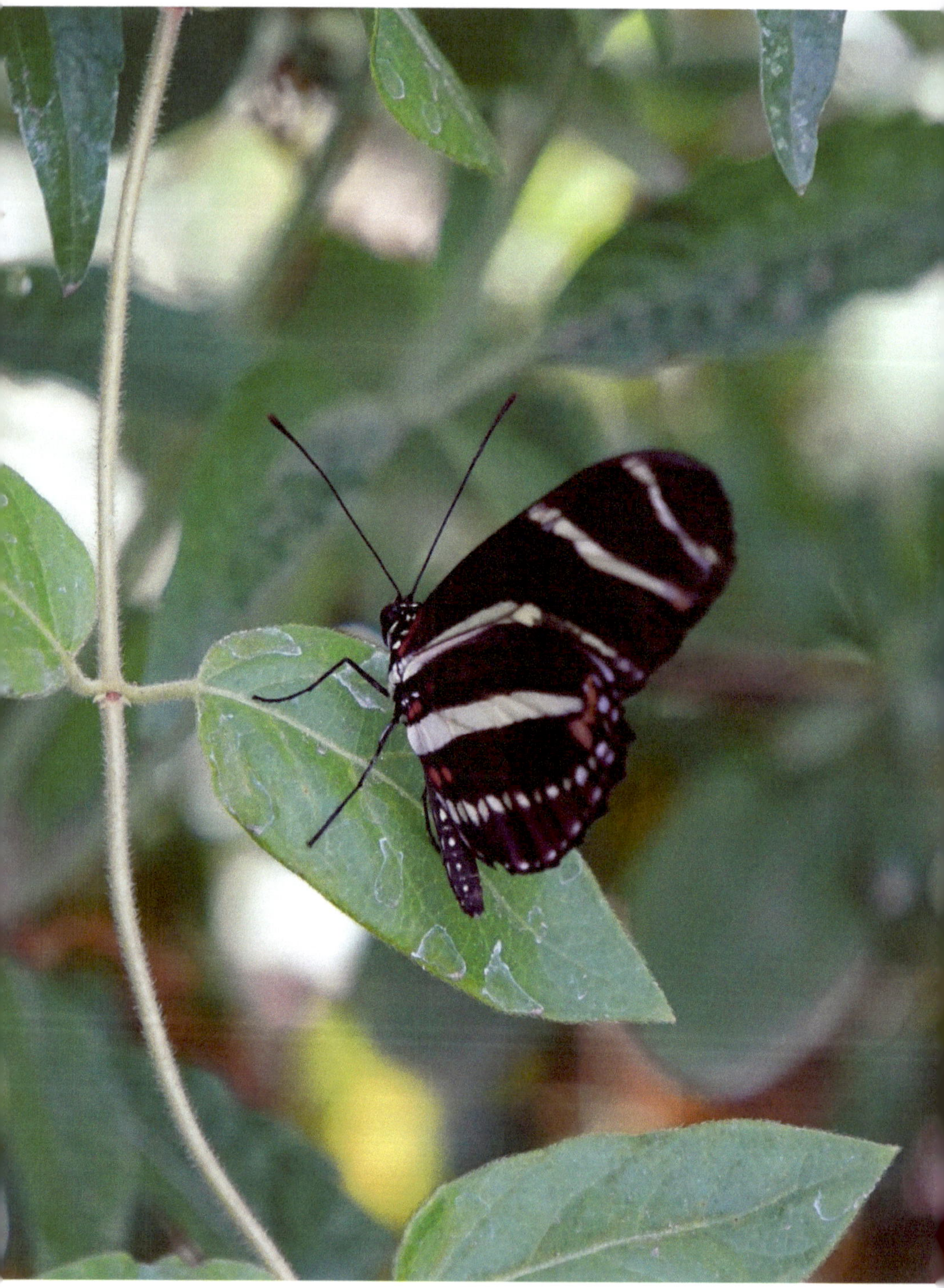

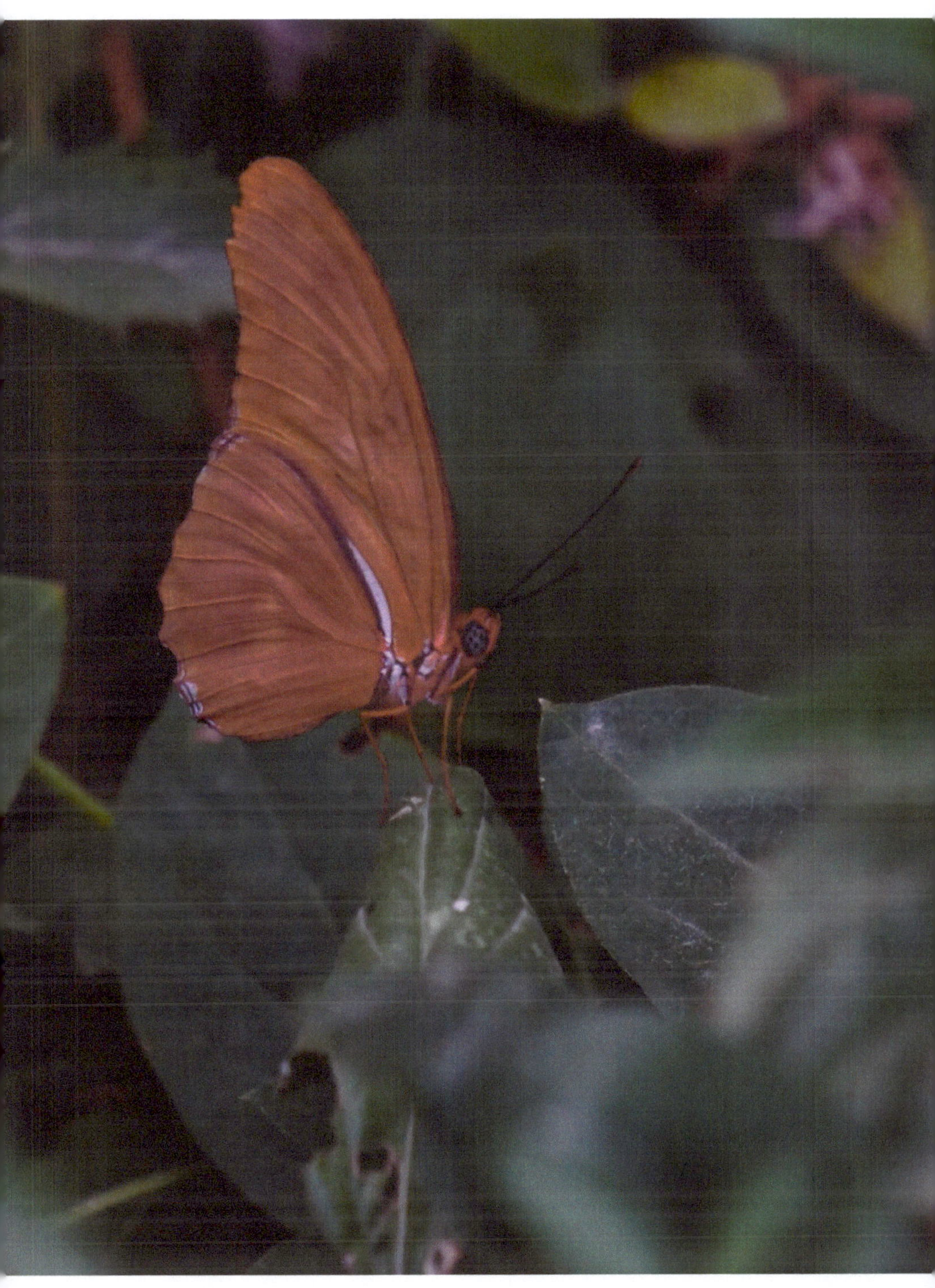

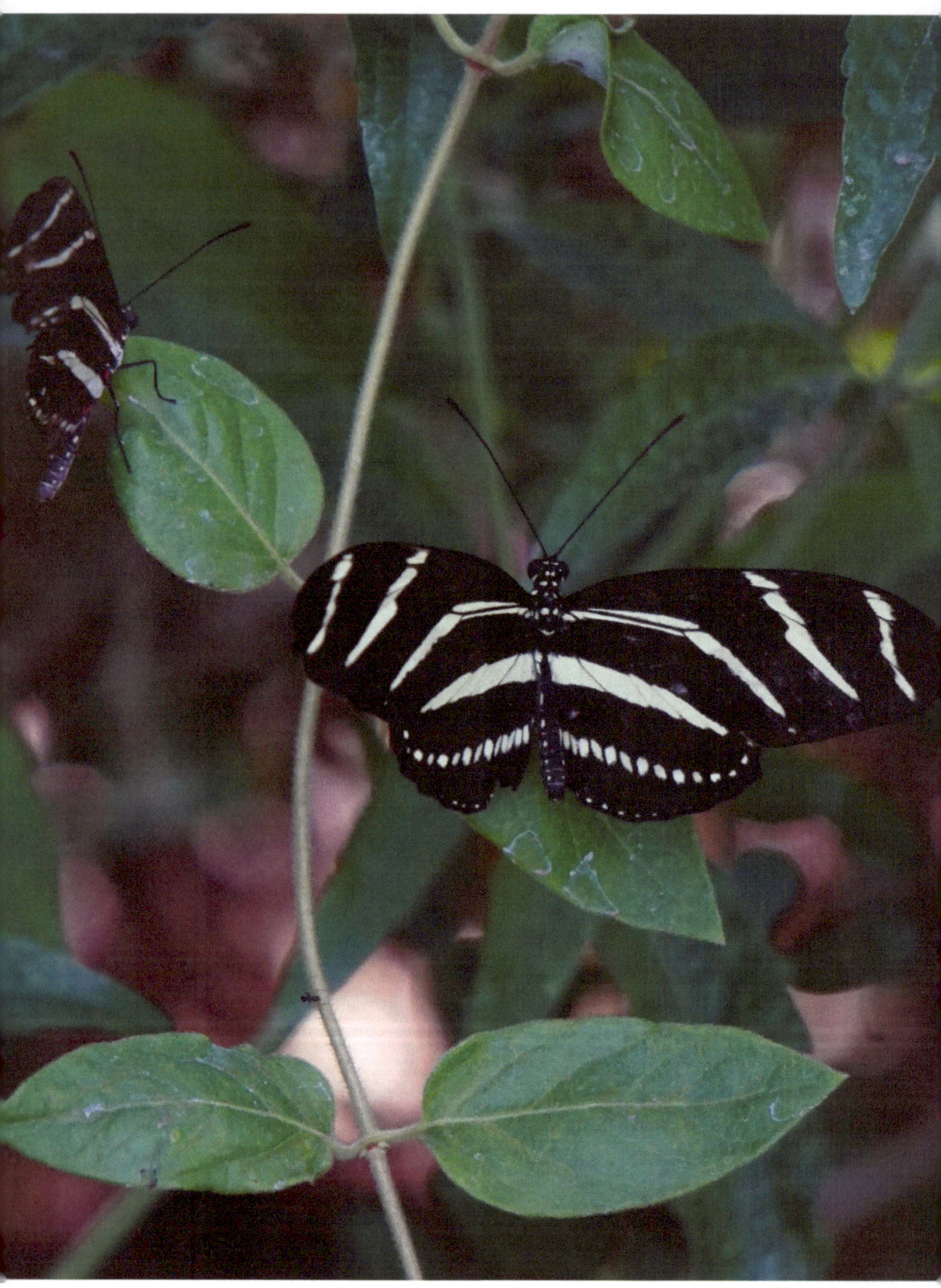

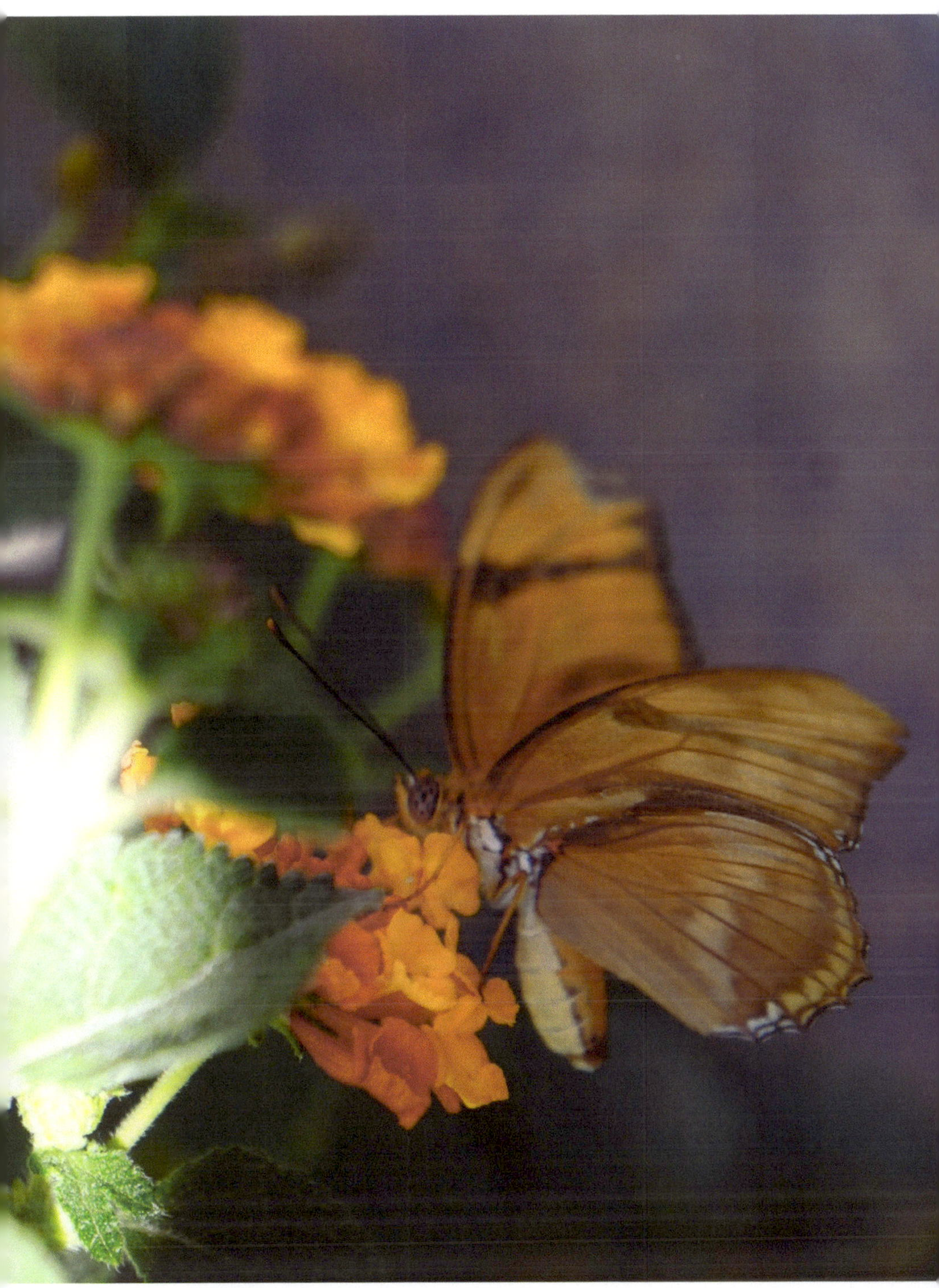

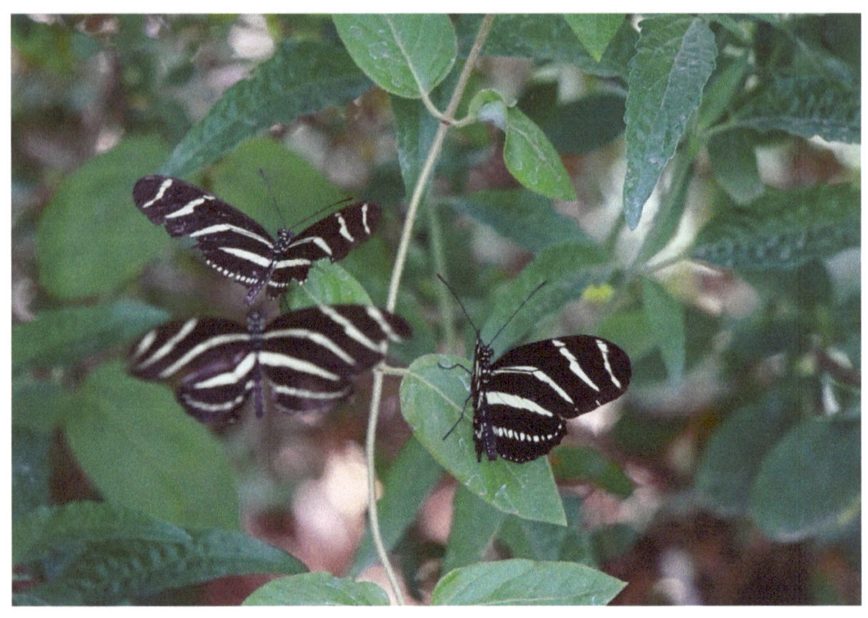

# Butterflies

Fliting and flying above the ground

Exploring the world all around

On an adventure through the sky

Only a dream until I fly